WALK WORTHY OF THE KINGDOM OF GOD

Stephen Kaung

ISBN: 978-1-942521-45-7

Available from:

Christian Testimony Ministry
4424 Huguenot Road
Richmond, Virginia 23235

www.christiantestimonyministry.com

Printed in USA

CONTENTS

Stephen Kaung spoke the messages contained in this booklet at the Northeast Christian Weekend Conference, Long Beach Island, New Jersey in October 2011. The spoken words have been transcribed by permission with only minimal editing for clarity. Unless otherwise indicated, Scripture quotations are from the New Translation by J. N. Darby.

WHAT IS THE KINGDOM OF GOD

I Thessalonians 2:12—and comfort and testify, that ye should walk worthy of God, who calls you to His own kingdom and glory.

THE BACKGROUND OF THE THESSALONICA LETTER

The Gospel Enters Europe

Our theme for this time is "Walk Worthy of God's Kingdom." We thank God for His presence. This is a critical time and we believe He is preparing us for His imminent return. May He speak to our hearts and by His grace enable us to walk worthy of His kingdom. Now, for some brothers and sisters who may not be familiar with the kingdom of God we will give a little background.

In Acts 15 we are told that Paul and Silas left Antioch for their second missionary trip, revisiting Phrygia and the Galatian countries. In Lystra they took Timothy with them to be an attendant. They were thinking of going to Asia, which is not Asia the continent but Asia Minor, a populous country; but strangely, the Holy Spirit forbade them. They continued on to Mysia and were thinking of going to Bithynia to preach the gospel, but again, the Spirit of Jesus forbade them. So they went straight until they reached Troas which was a coastal city. While in Troas Paul saw a vision—a Macedonian appeared to him and said, "Come and help us." So they decided it was the Lord's mind that they should go to Macedonia. They crossed the Aegean Sea, leaving Asia behind, and for the first time they entered into Europe. That is how Europe first received the gospel of Jesus Christ.

The Church at Philippi

They arrived in Philippi, which was a Roman colony, but they did not have ten men of leisure, which means there had to be ten Jewish men who were willing to form a synagogue. Hence, in that Roman colony there was no synagogue; but there were a few women who met together outside of the city for prayer. So Paul and his companions went to the river and joined these women who were praying, and Paul preached Christ Jesus to them. The Spirit of God touched the heart of Lydia, a woman who was in the business of selling purple, which at that time was a very high-class business. Lydia and her family turned to the Lord Jesus, and there was such love in her heart that she constrained Paul and his companions to stay with them.

During that time, Paul and his companions went out to pray, and as they were on the way a woman possessed by a demon followed them and cried, saying, "These are God's servants, and they are preaching the gospel of salvation." This continued on for several days, and Paul's heart was troubled because he did not want the devil mixed up with the Spirit of God so he turned around and cast that demon out. When the masters of this possessed woman saw that the hope of earning money was gone, they stirred up a turmoil and said, "These people came to preach what we Romans should not receive." Because of that, Paul and Silas were beaten and put into jail; but at midnight Paul and Silas prayed and sang songs to God. In the midst of their singing, there was an earthquake and all the doors of the jail were opened. The jailer awoke, and seeing that the doors were opened he thought all the prisoners were gone so he tried to kill himself. But Paul said, "We are here." So the jailer went in and asked them: "What must I do that I might be saved?" Paul replied: "Believe on the Lord Jesus, and thou shalt be saved and thy household." That night the jailer and his household believed and were baptized. The next morning when the officer said they could go, Paul said: "We are Romans and yet we were beaten and placed in prison without cause." Later, the officials came, apologized, and asked them to leave. So Paul and his companions left Philippi and went to Thessalonica.

Thessalonica

When they arrived in Thessalonica, they found more Jews there and a synagogue. Paul and his companions visited the synagogue and reasoned with the people how Christ must suffer first and rise from the dead, and this Christ is Jesus. Some of the Jews believed, but many of the Gentiles who worshiped in the synagogue believed, and not a few noble women. When these things happened, the Jews began to be jealous and they stirred up a mob. Because of that, they sent Paul and Silas away.

Eventually they went to Corinth, but in Paul's heart there was a longing to go back to Thessalonica because it was a young church of new believers who were suffering persecution from their own kinsmen and countrymen. Paul was so concerned for their spiritual condition that several times he wanted to go back but he was not allowed to. Finally, while he was in Corinth he sent Timothy to Thessalonica to visit those young Christians to see if they could stand through the persecutions. Timothy came back with the good news that these young Christians, in spite of persecutions from their own countrymen, were standing firm, waiting for the coming of the Lord and serving the living God. So Paul's heart was so comforted that he wrote the first letter to Thessalonica to further comfort them and to testify that they should walk worthy of God according as He had called them into His kingdom and glory. That is the background of this letter, and most likely it was written in 53 A.D.

THE GOSPEL OF THE KINGDOM

Mark 1:14-15—But after John was delivered up, Jesus came into Galilee preaching the glad tidings of the kingdom of God, and saying, The time is fulfilled and the kingdom of God has drawn nigh; repent and believe in the glad tidings.

Colossians 1:13—Who has delivered us from the authority of darkness, and translated us into the kingdom of the Son of his love.

We know that after John the Baptist was put in prison, the Lord Jesus began to preach the gospel in Galilee. He told them that the time had arrived and the kingdom of God was coming; therefore, they were to repent and believe in the glad tidings. This is the gospel that our Lord Jesus preached. Today, when we think of the gospel of Jesus Christ, probably our whole attention is upon this matter of having our sins forgiven and going to heaven. We call this the gospel of grace. But when our Lord Jesus began to preach the gospel, the emphasis was not on this but it is: "Repent for the kingdom of God has drawn nigh." In other words, He preached the gospel of the kingdom of God.

You will recall that in John 3 when Nicodemus—a rabbi and teacher in Israel—came to the Lord Jesus, he noticed that the Lord taught with authority. He came to visit our Lord at night and said, "We know you are a teacher from heaven." He was thinking about receiving more teaching although he had already had lots of teaching. He was a teacher himself, but he was hungry for more. Strangely, our Lord Jesus cut him off and said: "Unless you are born from above you cannot see the kingdom of God." Here was an educated man and a teacher of Israel, but he was seeking for the kingdom of God. Maybe in his mind he considered himself pretty near to the kingdom of God because he knew a lot, but he thought that was not enough. He was humble enough to come to the Lord Jesus to seek for more teaching about the kingdom of God. However, the Lord Jesus immediately said: "Unless you are born from above you cannot even see the kingdom of God much less enter in." This really surprised Nicodemus, so he said, "How can a person who has grown up go back into his mother's womb and be born again? That is impossible." The Lord Jesus said, "Verily, verily, I say unto you, unless you are born of the

7

Spirit, you cannot enter into the kingdom of God. For he that is born of the flesh is flesh and he that is born of the Spirit is spirit." So we find that in the conversation of the Lord Jesus with Nicodemus He was talking about the kingdom of God. If anyone wants to enter the kingdom of God, he must be born from above or born again. This is the gospel that our Lord Jesus preached.

GOD IS THE CENTER OF THE GOSPEL

This so great salvation that we find in Hebrews 2:3 was first preached by our Lord Himself, and it was affirmed by the apostles. God used signs and wonders and the distribution by the Holy Spirit to prove the reality of this gospel. It is a sad thing today that God's people, being so self-centered, are only thinking about what the gospel will do for them. If we believe in the Lord Jesus, our sins are forgiven, we have eternal life and heaven is guaranteed that even the Lord Himself surrounds us and we are the center. That is our selfish understanding of the gospel. But the gospel that our Lord Jesus and the apostles preached is the kingdom of God. In other words, God is the center; we are not the center.

When we believed in the Lord Jesus, God did something much more than we realized. In reading Ephesians 2 we find that before we believed in the Lord Jesus, we were dead in sins and transgressions. We followed the fashion or the current of the world; but behind the world we were under the authority and power of darkness. However, we did not realize that; we thought we were free and could do anything we wanted to. We thought we were the master not knowing that we were slaves to sin and to the enemy of God. We were under his control and tyranny. We were dead and considered as enemies of God. That was the situation before we believed in the Lord Jesus.

But thank God for His mercy! He sent His only beloved Son, the Lord Jesus, into this world to die. He shed His own blood and gave His life to us that we may be saved. It was during this time, as stated in Colossians 1:13, that God delivered us from the power of darkness and translated us into the kingdom of the Son of His love.

A New Position

When we believe in the Lord Jesus, there is so much that God has done for us. He has not only forgiven our sins, but He delivered us from eternal death. He justified us, He gave His own life to us, He gave us a new spirit and then sent the Holy Spirit to dwell in our new spirit and be responsible for our future. He did everything for us. He has delivered us from the power of darkness and has translated us into the kingdom of the Son of His love. In other words, our position has changed. Formerly, we were under the power of darkness—hopeless and helpless. We could do nothing but sin. We had no future and were destined to eternal death. Thank God, when He sent His Son to save us, He delivered us out of the power of darkness and translated us into the kingdom of the Son of His love—a new position. So this is what the gospel is. When we receive the gospel, it is more than a personal forgiveness of sin. It is more than receiving a life. It is a transfer of position. We are no longer under the power of darkness; today, we are in the kingdom of the Son of God's love.

A KINGDOM IS RULED BY THE KING

What does it mean to be in the kingdom of God? What is the kingdom? I believe this is something we should have a clear understanding of.

When the apostles were in Thessalonica, it was for a very short time; but during that time they labored for the Lord day and night, becoming an example before the Thessalonians. They were not at all in despair because of the sufferings they went through in Philippi. Instead, they endured the suffering. They forgot themselves and faithfully and patiently preached the gospel to the Thessalonians. What they did was more than some teaching about the kingdom; they set an example as to how to walk worthy of the kingdom of God. But first of all, we need to know what the kingdom of God is that we have been translated into.

The kingdom of God is probably difficult for us to understand because this country is a democracy and not a monarchy. Therefore, we do not have any experience of kingdom. In the Scriptures kingdom means a people within a certain sphere under the rulership of the king. The king is not only the sovereign of his kingdom but in a sense he is the kingdom because all the laws and rules of the kingdom come from him. The king makes the rules and has absolute authority over his people.

THE KINGDOM OF GOD IS FROM ETERNITY TO ETERNITY

Now, of course, we know in a very broad sense, the kingdom of God is from eternity to eternity because He is the One who created the universe. Therefore, His kingdom is from eternity to eternity. Everything is under His rule and control. Whether you believe in Him or obey Him does not matter. He is still the Sovereign of the universe. However, in a stricter sense, the kingdom of God means those people that are absolutely obedient to Him. They not only give allegiance to Him but even their very lives belong to Him. The King has absolute control over them.

God revealed to Nebuchadnezzar—the first great emperor of the Gentile nations—again and again that the heavens do rule. There is One who rules over the affairs of man, and He is the one who raises up kings and deposes them. He has absolute authority over the affairs of man. God Himself is the kingdom. He is the rule and has absolute authority over His people.

There is one place where it shows up very clearly what the kingdom of God is, and that is in I Chronicles 29. Towards the end of his reign David was preparing the material for the temple to be built, and it was in his affliction and affection that he had obtained much material to give to the Lord. Then he encouraged the people to do the same, and they began to give, preparing for the building the temple. Towards the end David prayed:

"And David blessed Jehovah in the sight of all the congregation; and David said, Blessed be thou, Jehovah, the God of our father Israel, for ever and ever. Thine, Jehovah, is the greatness, and the power, and the glory, and the splendour, and the majesty; for all that is in the heavens and on the earth is thine: thine, Jehovah, is the kingdom, and thou art exalted as Head above all; and riches and glory are of thee, and thou rulest over everything; and in thy hand is power and might; and in thy hand it is to make all great and strong. And now, our God, we thank thee, and praise thy glorious name" (I Chronicles 29:10-13).

In this praise, we find David saying, "Thine is the kingdom and Thou rulest over all. Riches and glory are of Thee, and in Thy hand is power and might; and in Thy hand it is to make all great and strong."

ABSOLUTE OBEDIENCE TO THE KING

What is the kingdom of God that God has transferred us into? This is our position today. We are in the kingdom of God, and it means one thing—we give our God absolute obedience. He is the ruler of His kingdom. It is His desire that we take up His own character that we may become faithful and true citizens of the kingdom of God.

THE KINGDOM OF GOD IS THE KINGDOM OF THE SON OF HIS LOVE

Then we find in Colossians 1:13 that God has transferred us out of the power of darkness into the kingdom of the Son of His love. What is the kingdom of God? The kingdom of God is the kingdom of the Son of His love. They are one and the same because this is related to the eternal purpose of God. Even before the foundation of the world, even before God began to create anything, God made a decision according to His good pleasure (see Ephesians 1:9). God has a good pleasure. There is one thing that pleases Him more than anything else, and that is His only begotten Son. All of God's thoughts are about His Son; therefore, He wanted to give everything to His Son. He created the universe for His Son, and He wanted His Son to sum up all things in heaven and on earth. That simply means that everything in heaven and earth will speak, will manifest, will glorify, and show forth His Son. That is the eternal purpose of God.

MAN IS THE LIFE-COMPANION OF GOD'S SON

In the eternal purpose of God, He included man in a special way because He gave man to His only begotten Son to be His life-companion. This is such a glorious thought! Who are we? If you think of size, how can we compare to even a little hill? We are like the dust of the earth because we are made of dust. Yet it is the good pleasure of our God to make us the life-companion of His beloved Son.

Of course, in order to be His life-companion, this is not a simple thing. There must be a correspondence and a likeness. There must be an agreement between His beloved Son and us. How can we, who are full of flesh, become the life-companion of our Lord Jesus who is full of the Holy Spirit? We are so unqualified. Nevertheless, we are called into His kingdom that through the life He has given to us and the Holy Spirit who dwells in us to teach us and transform us, we may be delivered from everything that is not like His Son or contradictory to His Son. This is done in order for us to be remade, as it were, with His Son's character and life. One day we will be suitable for His beloved Son. This is the kingdom of the Son of His love. He has put us in that position, and what a glorious position that is!

When we think about this, will it make us ashamed of ourselves and be willing to deny ourselves, take up our cross and follow the Lord? This is God's way to transform us. We should thank God for all of the discipline, difficulties, sufferings, tribulations, and troubles that we have gone through in life. I often think that after the Lord saved me, the best thing He could have done was to take me to Himself. Then I would be free from all of the troubles of these long years, but God knows better.

What will you be if you are full of yourself and have very little of Christ? If you are not growing in the Lord, if you are not taking up His character and being transformed, when you come to His presence, He will say, "Unfit." No wonder the five foolish virgins, when they could not enter into the marriage feast and they were cast into outer darkness, were gnashing their teeth and repenting for their foolishness. This is the kingdom of God. It is the kingdom of the Son of God's love. As God loves His beloved Son He loves us with the same love. He gave His only begotten Son to us that we may be like Him. Do you want to be like God's Son that He may be the firstborn among many brethren and lead many sons to glory? Now this is God's glorious purpose for us.

THE KINGDOM OF THE HEAVENS

What is the kingdom of God? Matthew used a different term: he called it the kingdom of the heavens. "Repent for the kingdom of the heavens has drawn nigh" (3:2b). "Blessed are those who are empty in themselves for theirs is the kingdom of God. Blessed are those who hunger and thirst for righteousness, because they will be filled. Blessed are those who are pure in heart, for they shall see God" (see Matthew 5). This kingdom is also called the kingdom of the heavens. In a sense this is especially related to Christians. If you want to know the difference between the kingdom of the heavens and the kingdom of God, broadly speaking they are one. Strictly speaking, the kingdom of the heavens is part of the kingdom of God because the kingdom of God is from eternity to eternity. But the kingdom of the heavens came to this earth at the first coming of the Lord Jesus. Before the Lord came, John the Baptist, His forerunner, preached,

"Repent for the kingdom of the heavens has drawn nigh." In other words, it was not here yet. But strangely, when our Lord Jesus preached, He said the same thing: "Repent for the kingdom of the heavens has drawn nigh." The King had come but He had no kingdom at that time; He had no people yet. Through the preaching of the Lord Jesus and the discipling of the people who believed in Him, He then said in Matthew 11: "The kingdom of the heavens is to be seized by violence and the violent seizes upon it" (see v. 12). In other words, the Lord Jesus had come. The King was here and He had gathered around Him some people. So He said: "The kingdom of the heavens is here." Who will be able to seize that kingdom? It will be those who do violence to themselves. We do not like the word violence because of the bad connotation we have of it. But actually, the word violence is neutral. In other words, if you do violence to other people, that is sin. If you do violence to yourself for the kingdom's sake, now that is glory.

LIVING IN THE KINGDOM OF THE HEAVENS

What do you mean by violence? Violence simply means deny yourself. Peter denied the Lord three times, but he denied the wrong person. He should have denied himself. Who are we denying today? Do we deny ourselves, take up the cross daily and follow Him? The cross simply means that when God's thoughts and our thoughts cross each other, when His mind and our mind go in different directions, when our feelings and His feelings conflict, will we keep ourselves? Or, will we deny ourselves, take up the cross, and follow the Lord? In doing that, while we are living on this earth we will not only be in the kingdom of God but we will be living in the kingdom of God literally and spiritually. We will be loyal citizens of that kingdom, and the heavens rule over us.

Who is ruling over you today? Are the heavens ruling over you or are you still the ruler of your own life? I think this is something very serious, and we really need to be before the Lord about it. You will recall when our Lord Jesus was judged by Pilate in John 19, he asked Him: "Are you a King?" And He said, "Yes, I was born a King, but My kingdom is not of this world. If My kingdom were of this world, My people would fight for Me, but My kingdom is not of this world. I have come to bear witness to the truth."

The kingdom of the heavens is different from the earth. The Lord Jesus told His disciples: "Those who rule on earth or those in authority will sit high up, give commands, and let other people serve them. Not so among you. Those who are great among you shall be the least. Those who are to be high need to be low. I have come not to be served, but to serve, and to give My life as a ransom for all" (see Matthew 20:25-28). The way of heaven is very different from the way of this world. That is why while we live on this earth, if we are under the rule of heaven, then we will be able to live a heavenly life just like the Lord Jesus. He was in this world but He was not of this world. This is the same way we should be.

THE KINGDOM OF GOD IS A SPIRITUAL KINGDOM

Righteousness

What is the kingdom of God? The kingdom of God is a spiritual kingdom. We find in Romans 14:17: "For the kingdom of God is not eating and drinking, but righteousness, and peace, and joy in the Holy Spirit." This tells us that the kingdom of God is a spiritual kingdom. It is not in eating and drinking. This world is focused on eating and drinking. What shall I eat? What shall I drink? What shall I be dressed with? How can I have a rich life and enjoy all the pleasures of this world? That is the world; however the kingdom of God is not of this world. It is not composed of eating and drinking but of righteousness. God is righteous. Therefore, those who are the Lord's must practice righteousness.

Thank God, even though we were once unrighteous and condemned by God, He has saved us. He forgave our sins and clothed us with Christ Jesus. He is our robe that covers our nakedness so that we have a standing before God. We are justified in the sight of God.

22

Nevertheless, that is not enough. We who have been justified not only need to walk righteously, we need to practice righteousness. There are many things we can do and many places we can go that in the sight of man we will not be condemned. But our God has a higher standard. We have to satisfy Him who is altogether righteous. In I John we are told that we need to practice righteousness which means to do everything right in the sight of God. How do we know? Thank God, the Holy Spirit dwells in us. He is our teacher, not only in big things, but even in small things. He will teach us in all things, and if we obey the teaching of the Anointing, we will abide in Christ. That is the way we will know that we are right in the sight of God.

Peace

In this world, there is no peace. The Lord Jesus is our peace; therefore, we not only have peace with God, we have peace with one another. So if there is anything we hold against our brother or sister, we need to forgive knowing that we who have been forgiven much, how can we hold anything against those who may offend us just a little? In a sense, it is good discipline for us. That is the kingdom of God—that in our conscience there is no regret. It is as Paul said: "Before God and man I maintain a conscience without offense" (see Acts 24:16). That does not mean that I am perfect, but at least I do whatever the Spirit of God touches my conscience with, and there is peace. So we discover how the apostle Paul had peace within himself in all kinds of circumstance

Joy of the Holy Spirit

Real joy comes from God. People may seek for happiness but that is only superficial. Joy comes from God. The joy of the Lord is our strength. Thank God, oftentimes when we are passing through great difficulties, strangely, deep within our heart there is joy. Our Lord Jesus was like that. You remember how He had labored so diligently and so faithfully in Capernaum, in Chorazin, and in other places, and they still did not believe. In that environment it was the most desperate situation, but the Lord Jesus lifted His head and said: "Thank You, Father, for this is Your good pleasure to reveal

Thy mind to the babes but to the prudent and the wise Thou has hidden it" (see Matthew 11:25). Joy in the Holy Spirit. You may shed tears but deep within there is joy knowing that the Lord is with you and He is pleased with you.

These are a few explanations of what the kingdom of God is. Thank God, He has translated us out of the power of darkness. But where are we today? We are in the kingdom of God. Therefore, should we not behave like the sons of the kingdom? May the Lord help us!

Shall we pray:

Dear Lord, what can we say? Thou hast done something so tremendous and so glorious that we can never get ourselves out or get ourselves in, but Thou hast done it. We praise and thank Thee for Thy beloved Son. Through Calvary's cross Thou hast transferred us out of the power of darkness into the kingdom of the Son of Thy love. Oh dear God, we thank Thee for the glorious position that Thou hast placed us. Now Lord, work it out in each and every one of us, that we may walk worthy of Thy kingdom to the praise of Your glory. We ask in Thy precious name. Amen.

HOW TO WALK WORTHY OF THE KINGDOM OF GOD

I Thessalonians 4:3a—For this is the will of God, even your sanctification.

I Thessalonians 4:7—For God has not called us to uncleanness, but in sanctification.

I Thessalonians 5:16-18—Rejoice always; pray unceasingly; in everything give thanks, for this is the will of God in Christ Jesus towards you.

Let's have a word of prayer:

Dear Lord, as we are gathered here, our hearts are full of gratitude as we remember Thee at Thy table. Lord, we see our unworthiness but we praise and thank Thee because we see more of Thy worthiness. Who are we that Thou should look upon us and should love us even to the uttermost? Oh, dear Lord, Thou hast touched our hearts. We are Thine forever, and we are willing by Thy grace to follow Thee all the way. Whatever Thy purpose may be in our lives, Lord, bring it to pass that

Thou mayest be glorified. We thank Thee for giving us this opportunity of sharing Thy Word. Thy Word is life, living and operative, and we trust Thy Holy Spirit to quicken Thy Word to our hearts. May Thy Word be our life that Thou mayest be glorified. We commit this time into Thy hand, trusting in Thy working. We ask in Thy name. Amen.

We have been considering this matter of the kingdom of God. The kingdom of God is where God rules and His sovereignty is respected and obeyed. It takes its character from Himself—who God is, what God is, and what the nature of His kingdom is. The kingdom of God is called the kingdom of the Son of God's love. It is the same because God's purpose is centered upon His only begotten Son. He has given the kingdom to His Son and made His Son the King of kings and Lord of lords. We are to obey Him and submit ourselves absolutely to His rule. The kingdom of God is not of this world but of the heavens because in His kingdom the heavens do rule over the affairs of man. The Lord Jesus said: "My kingdom is not of this world, but I come to bear witness of the truth." The kingdom of God is a spiritual kingdom. It is not in eating and drinking but it is in righteousness, peace, and the joy in the Holy Spirit.

When we believe in the Lord Jesus, at first, probably our whole thought is centered upon what He has done for me and what I have received from Him. This is our emphasis. But when our Lord Jesus began to preach the gospel, it was the gospel of the kingdom of God. Even after His resurrection and during the forty days that He appeared to His disciples, He talked to them about the kingdom of God. He is the One who commenced this message. But we find that the apostles who followed reinforced it. And God used miracles, wonders, and the distribution of the Holy Spirit to support it. So the gospel as we discover in the word of God is a so great salvation. It is something that our Lord preached, and His apostles and disciples preached. This is the gospel we *must* proclaim.

A NEW POSITION

When we were saved, something happened that was far more than personal. Before we were saved we were in sins and transgressions and followed the fashion of this world. We could not help it because behind the world is the power of darkness that rules and controls everyone. We were enemies of God which was our position before we believed in the Lord Jesus. But thank God, He has transferred us out of the kingdom of darkness into the kingdom of the Son of His love (see Colossians 1:13). Therefore, when we believe in the Lord Jesus, there is something more than what we have personally gained in believing in the Lord. There is a change in position. God has delivered us out of the power of darkness just as God saved the children of Israel when He delivered them out from the tyranny of Pharaoh. He transferred them into the land flowing with milk and honey. So in like manner, as we believe in the gospel, God did the same thing to us. Our position today is no longer under the power of darkness. We have been positionally transferred into the kingdom of the Son of God's love.

POSSESSING THE KINGDOM

Position is one thing but possession is another thing. Position gives us the possibility or the potential, but possession is the real inheritance. So when God transferred us into the kingdom of the Son of His love, what is in His heart? He does not want us just to have a position; He wants us to possess the kingdom. He wants us to be transformed and conformed to the image of His beloved Son that we may enter into our inheritance. It is like the children of Israel—God had promised them the land of Canaan but they had to go in and put their feet down which then became the place that belonged to them. In the same manner we are not to think that because we have the position in the kingdom of God that His kingdom is ours. It is promised to us. It is supposed to be our inheritance but there is something more that is necessary. We have to put our feet down, tread upon it, and claim it in order to possess it.

WALKING IN THE KINGDOM

The emphasis this time is on walking worthy of God's kingdom. Now when we read the word *walk*, it immediately gives us the impression that this is not a position, but is based on a position and we start walking in it. And that is experience. So it does not mean that because we have been given that position in the kingdom of God, automatically the kingdom of God is ours. We may have it, and we are meant to have it. That is God's will for us, but we can lose it. We can miss it.

In the story of Esau and Jacob, we recall that Esau was born first; therefore he had the right of the firstborn. We know that among the Jews at that time, the right of the firstborn was very important because he was to be the priest of the family. He was to continue the promises of God to Abraham. He had the double portion of the inheritance which was his right; it belonged to him. Unfortunately, even though Esau had the position of the firstborn, he lost it for a cup of lentil soup. He despised the firstborn right. Even afterwards when he wept and cried, he could not regain it. So there is the glorious hope presented to every one of us of the privilege of possessing our possession. We have the privilege of the firstborn sons, but it does not mean it is automatically ours. We need to walk worthy of God's kingdom.

KEEPING THE SERMON ON THE MOUNT

Now of course, we know in order to walk worthy of God's kingdom, it is something beyond us. Some people take the Sermon on the Mount as a higher law and think they must keep it like the children of Israel. God gave them the Ten Commandments, the Law, and said: "Thou shalt, thou shalt not. You must keep it. If you do, then you are My people, and I am your God." It was conditional. Somehow this kind of impression is deep in our thoughts. We think that in order to gain the kingdom, in order to walk worthy of the kingdom, we must try our very best and then we may get it. If we do not try, then certainly we will not have it.

When I was a teenager in the 1930's, I recall a movement that started from England and spread all over the world, even going to China. It was called the Oxford Group movement which was different from the Oxford movement. It was founded by Frank Buchman. They took the Sermon on the Mount as their objective and emphasized four absolutes. I have forgotten three of them, but the one I remember was absolute purity. They tried to live a life according to the Sermon on the Mount— absolutely pure, absolutely honest, and absolutely real. When it came to China, a number of Christians among the upper class joined them. One man who was well known and respected in China in Christian literature joined it. Later on, during the war time, we met in Chongqing. Even though he was much older than I, he shared with me his heart. He was a very honest person and well respected. He told me that every time he was physically weak all his past sins came back to him and bothered him. He had to confess all his sins again and again in order to get peace. This was a tortured soul. I tried to share with him the preciousness of the blood of our Lord Jesus. Once we are cleansed, it is forever cleansed. God said, "I will forgive and forget." Somehow this could not register in his mind. What a pity!

If we do not try to keep the Sermon on the Mount, probably we will feel better and even deceive ourselves into thinking that we are better than anyone else; we are okay. Once we try to follow the Sermon on the Mount or try to keep it, it will kill us. In a very real sense, the kingdom of God is so heavenly, so spiritual, so of God, so of Christ Jesus that it is beyond anybody's ability to keep the law.

TO WALK WORTHY OF THE KINGDOM IS BY GRACE

First of all, we need to be very clear: to walk worthy of God's kingdom is not to walk by our own strength, by ourselves. Formerly, we used ourselves to commit sins. Then we changed and said we will use our own flesh to keep the law of God. Try it. Nobody can. As the Bible said, this is something impossible with man, but that does not mean it is impossible with God. So to walk worthy of God's kingdom is a matter of grace. Grace begins and ends our spiritual life. From the very first day we believe in the Lord Jesus to the very last day when we shall see Him face to face, it is grace—grace upon grace.

THE WORK OF CHRIST AND THE HOLY SPIRIT MAKES OUR EXPERIENCE PERSONAL

What the Lord Jesus did on Calvary's cross has given us the position. He said, "It is finished."

That means there is nothing left to be done. So far as God's salvation is concerned, everything has been done. We cannot add to it nor take anything from it. The work Christ did has given us the position. He has translated us into His kingdom. But in order for what Christ did two thousand years ago outside of Jerusalem at Calvary to become what He is doing in you and me today, making it our personal experience, it has to be transferred, as it were, applied, and become operative in our lives by the Holy Spirit. That is the experience.

What Christ did on Calvary's cross is objective truth, the whole truth and nothing but the truth. You cannot take away from it nor can you add to it. That is the salvation that our Lord Jesus has done for us. He that is born of the Spirit is spirit. But after we are saved, God not only renews our spirit He even puts His own Spirit into our spirit. He is there to do the work of transferring or translating what has been done by Christ two thousand years ago into our very being. It becomes our daily experience. Christ becomes real and living to us. It enables us to say as Paul said: "For me to live is Christ."

This is the work of the Holy Spirit. By the two works—one by the Son of God and one by the Holy Spirit—we enter into our possession. That is the way we can walk worthy of God's kingdom.

PAUL'S MINISTRY WAS AS A NURSE

Now having said that, we will look at how Paul comforted and testified to those young Christians in Thessalonica. We know that Paul was a Pharisee but he did not instruct or help those young Christians in Thessalonica as a Pharisee; that is to say, as someone who sits on the throne and will not move even his finger to do what he instructs and commands as law for the people to do. That is the way the Pharisees taught people but not the Lord Jesus nor Paul. In the first letter to the Thessalonians he mentioned that when he was among them, he was like a nurse (see 2:7). He was not like a teacher but a nurse and there is a great difference between the two. Now a nurse also teaches the children, but primarily she nurses the children. She brings them up, sharing her life with them, and she enables them to grow up.

PAUL'S MINISTRY WAS AS A FATHER

Paul also mentioned that when he was among them, he was like a father to them (see 2:11-12). There is a difference between how the father teaches his children and how a teacher instructs them. A father is supposed to bring up his children in the admonition and discipline of the Lord; therefore, he sets an example before his children in the way he lives. Whatever way he instructs his children or when he disciplines them, he is the model or the example. That is the reason the children will obey. If the father does not set the example and tries to teach the children, then the children will say, "What about you?" That is the difference.

We find that when the apostle Paul instructed, helped, or testified to those young Christians in Thessalonica, actually he set himself as an example before them. Even though his days with them were short, yet when we read I Thessalonians, we see how he lived among them and how he worked with his own hands. He did not want to be any trouble for them; therefore he set himself as an example before them. He loved them and was willing to give his own life to them. Within such a short time he had left such an impression upon the Thessalonian believers, it is no wonder they followed his example. We learn from this that we cannot teach people like a Pharisee; it will not work. We have to teach them as a nurse and a father.

When our Lord Jesus was on earth, this was the way He taught His disciples. He set an example before them. Whatever He said is what He is. That is the reason when the disciples heard what Jesus said, they believed and followed Him.

WALK ACCORDING TO THE LIFE IN US

How do we walk worthy of the kingdom of God? Walk is something that we do day by day. It is not a hundred-meter dash. It is a daily, continuous going on. That means after we are saved and transferred into the kingdom of God, we are to walk patiently, continuously, constantly, without ceasing, according to the way of the kingdom. To walk in the way of the kingdom is not something that we can do by ourselves. We are to walk according to the life of Christ that is within us. He walks with us and talks with us. That is the way that we may walk worthy of God's kingdom.

SANCTIFICATION

As we read I Thessalonians, we discover a few things that the apostle Paul mentioned especially to the Thessalonian believers. First, in chapter 4:3 he said: "For this is the will of God, even your sanctification."

Again he said: "You are not called to uncleanness, but in sanctification" (see 4:7). So after we have been justified, God expects us to be holy as He is holy. That is our walk. We cannot walk anymore like the people of this world. We cannot try to befriend the world, to seek the things of the world, the lust of the flesh, the lust of the eyes, and the pride of life. This is not only a trap to young people but also to the older ones. However, we often hear young people say, "You old people, you have already experienced the world, but we have not. Just let us try it." Love not the world, nor the things of the world. If we love the things of the world, the love of the Father is not in us.

Sanctification simply means to be holy. To be holy simply means to be separated from the world and separated unto God. That is holiness.

Called Saints

Thank God, when we believe in the Lord Jesus, in a sense, He has already sanctified us. In I Corinthians I Paul wrote to the Corinthian believers and said: "To those sanctified in Christ Jesus, called saints." Today, if anyone called you saint, what will be your reaction? You will probably say, "I am not good." It is because the Catholic Church has made people so-called saints. When those so-called saints were living in this world, they lived so piously that they accumulated so much merit it not only helped them to go to heaven, but they had more to spare. Therefore, if one said a rosary for the saint who has died, he can spare some of his merits to get that one out of purgatory faster. Recently, they were trying to make a pope a saint. To qualify for sainthood they said he had to have done a few miracles after he died and then he could be entitled to be called a saint.

We find in the Bible that we are called saints because we have been sanctified by God. In other words, God has already set us apart from the world unto Himself. We belong to Him; therefore, we belong to another world—the kingdom of God. Our position is a sanctified position; therefore, should we live an unclean life, unsanctified, unholy life? Will it not be a contradiction?

Thank God, He is not only the One who gives us the position but with the position He has made every provision for us to make it our possession. God has already given us all things concerning life and godliness. He has given to us all the precious promises that we may be able to become partakers of His divine nature and be delivered from our flesh.

The Three Parts of Man to be Sanctified

In I Thessalonians 5 we read these words: "Now the God of peace himself sanctify you wholly: and your whole spirit, and soul, and body be preserved blameless at the coming of our Lord Jesus. He is faithful who calls you, who will also perform it" (vvs. 23-24).

So we need to experience sanctification or holiness, and being set apart for God day by day, hour by hour, minute by minute, that our whole being—spirit, soul, and body—be sanctified.

Now according to God's order of man, he is made of three parts. There is the spirit which enables him to communicate with God the Spirit. That is the reason man can worship God in spirit and in truth. Then God gave man a soul; he became a living soul. Our soul makes us conscience of ourselves. We have feeling/emotion, mind/thought, and will/volition. These faculties represent our soul. They make us what we are. We have a personality that makes us different from everyone else. I often say we have a soul shape just like we have a body shape. Everybody is different because every soul is different. We have a certain shape that represents each as an individual. Then of course, we have a body. The body is made up of the dust of the earth;

therefore, it is in contact with the world and its surroundings. Through the five senses we are in touch with the world.

The Bible tells us that salvation is not something that happens only once and that is all. In other words, when you are saved, it does not mean that your whole being is saved. What does it mean when we talk about a person being saved? To put it strictly, it simply means that he that is born of the Spirit is spirit. You are born from above, and your dead spirit that was dead in sins and transgressions and cut off from God is now cleansed and renewed by the blood of our Lord Jesus. It is a new spirit before God. So our new spirit and the Holy Spirit within cries together to God: "Abba Father." Do you know you have a new spirit? Do you know the Holy Spirit is dwelling in your spirit? And do you know Christ is the life of your spirit?

When a person is saved, is he totally changed? No. Was your body changed when you were saved from a mortal body to an immortal body? No. This is still the same body that is open to the attack of bacteria, sin, and death. Well, there was a superficial change; a long face becomes a round face, but that is superficial. Very soon that long face will reappear. As long as we live in this world, we still live in this old body. But thank God, Romans 8 tells us that one day this mortal body will be changed into an immortal body. And I Corinthians 15 tells us the same thing: this corruptible body will become incorruptible. We will take on a new spiritual body just like the body that our Lord Jesus took up when He was resurrected. Wonderful! So we have yet to be saved.

The Body is the Temple of the Holy Spirit

During this time, while we are still in this mortal body, how are we going to deal with our body? How are we going to use our body? How are we going to walk worthy of God's kingdom? In I Corinthians 6:19-20 we are told that this body, even though it is still a mortal body, is the temple of the Holy Spirit. The Holy Spirit has come to live in us. This body is no longer ours because we have been bought with a price. Who bought us? God bought us. What was the price? His only beloved Son. He paid the highest price to redeem our bodies. We are not our own, we are His; therefore, glorify God in your body. So do not treat your body as if it is your own. It is no longer your own. Even this old body, this corruptible body, this fading body, belongs to God. He is the owner, and He expects us to glorify Him in this body.

The apostle Paul says in I Corinthian 9 that we are in a race. We are to fight, but not as one who beats the air. We need to discipline our body. He says, "I keep my body underneath me." To put it very vividly: "I beat my body black and blue lest after having preached to others, I myself become a castaway" (see vvs. 26-27). In other words, this body tries to rule over us, but we should rule over our body. We should not listen to the lust of the body. We should listen to the Holy Spirit and even beat our body black and blue. In other words, we do not allow our body to be our owner.

People in this world live for their body: What shall I eat? What shall I drink? But we are to seek the kingdom of God first and His righteousness, and all these things shall be added unto us. How do we live our lives today? Are we still indulging ourselves? Are we still living for our body? Or are we truly living to glorify God even in this mortal body? This was what Paul did, and he encouraged the young Thessalonian Christians to do likewise.

Again I say, it is not by our own strength. Who does not love his own body? Who does not care for his body? It is only the love of God and the grace of God that enables us to put our body under that we may glorify God. One small example is this: One battle is between you and your bed—whether you are able to rise up early in order to spend time with the Lord or whether you love your body so much that you will roll over in your bed. Now I wonder how many brothers and sisters are still in that battle. Are you losing or winning? That is our body. One day, this body will take up immortality and incorruptibility, and become a spiritual body that will live forever and ever. Only at that moment will we be able to live for God without any problems.

The Inward War within our Soul and Body

This is a battle to the end. Not only were we delivered from the great death—that is, our spirit was born again—but we are being delivered today. In other words, salvation is going on in our soul today. Even after we have believed in the Lord Jesus and He came and dwelt in our spirit to become our life, there is yet the old life remaining in our soul. In other words, Christ is the life in our spirit, but self is the life in our soul. There is still the selfish self, fallen self, self-centered self, having many opinions, many ideas, many reasonings, many resistances because the flesh is an enemy of the spirit. It cannot obey God nor can it understand God. It is an enemy of God.

After we are saved we find that there is an inward war going on within us. There are two lives within us. The life of Christ tells us one thing and the life of self tells us another thing. Unfortunately, as Philip Melanchon, the theologian of the Reformation, said: "The old Adam is too much for young Melachon." And Martin Luther said the same thing: "I am not afraid of the pope or cardinals, kings and rulers, but I am afraid of the tyrant within me." Do you have such feelings? Is it not that which seems to hinder your spiritual growth? That is the reason why our Lord Jesus seems to be so unreasonable when He said: "He that loves his father, mother, brother or sister, children, even his own life more than Me cannot be My disciple." If we mind our own mind, we cannot be His disciple. If we will our own will, we cannot be His disciple. In other words, our soul has to be saved to be purified. Hence, this process of sanctification is going on day by day without ceasing.

The Salvation of the Soul

Whenever the Holy Spirit in our spirit tells us one thing and the self-life in our soul insists on another, a cross is made. That is the time to see whether we are willing to deny ourselves, take up the cross, and follow the Lord. If we cannot, then we cannot be the disciples of the Lord Jesus. But by the grace of God and the love of God, if we are willing to deny ourselves, take up the cross and follow Him daily, then our soul is being saved.

He that saves his life today for himself shall lose it, but he that loses his soul-life for My sake and the gospel's sake shall gain it to eternity. That is what we find in I Peter which is called the salvation of the soul (see 1:9). Many Christians know only the initial salvation of their spirit, but they do not know the saving of their soul or their body. God's salvation is perfect. The cross cannot be separated from the Christian just like the cross cannot be separated from Christ. If we have a cross-less Christ, we have no Christ at all. If we are a cross-less Christian, we are not living as a Christian. Praise God, to us this is impossible, but to Him all things are possible. When the love of Christ constrains us, we will refuse to live for ourselves and live for Him. It is grace—grace upon grace.

What about our spirit? Can our spirit be contaminated? Yes. That is why Paul said in II Corinthians: "Purify your flesh and spirit in the fear of God" (see 7:1). The influence of our soul can penetrate into our spirit and make our spirit mixed and impure. Do not allow any influence from outside or from your soul to penetrate or invade your spirit so that you may obey God with your whole heart. Thank God, this is the work that God said He will do by the Holy Spirit who dwells in us. However, it requires our cooperation, our yielding to Him, and our obedience. Are you willing to do that? Be ye holy for He is holy.

ABOUNDING IN LOVE TOWARD ONE ANOTHER

The second thing is found in I Thessalonians 3:12-13: "But you, may the Lord make to exceed and abound in love toward one another, and toward all, even as we also towards you, in order to the confirming of your hearts unblamable in holiness before our God and Father at the coming of our Lord Jesus with all his saints."

Even though the church in Thessalonica was a young church, they were known for their love for God, for their labor of love, and for the love of the brethren. But Paul did not praise them and say, "Now you have reached the goal." No, he could not say that because love has no end. God is love. If their love was from Him, there was no limit to that love. The Bible said, "Owe no one anything, except to love one another" (see

Romans 13:8). There will never come a day when you can say, "I have loved enough. I have loved God enough." Nor can you say, "I have loved my brothers and sisters enough. That is enough. No more." That is not love because love never ends. Our love is limited and self-centered. Our love always finds a reason to love; but God's love is unlimited with no reason. He loves because He loves (see Deuteronomy 7:7-8). Sometimes we hear people boast of their love which makes you wonder if it is natural love like Peter or if it is divine love like Christ. So we shall never be satisfied or be proud of loving; we shall always feel we do not love enough. We do not love God enough nor do we love our brothers and sisters enough. Love knows no end. So let us go on.

THREE THINGS THAT CANNOT BE MISSING TO WALK WORTHY

Thirdly, we find in I Thessalonians 5:16 these three things: "Rejoice always; pray unceasingly; in everything give thanks, for this is the will of God in Christ Jesus towards you." There are three ingredients here that cannot be missing if we are to walk worthy in God's kingdom.

Rejoice Always

How can I always rejoice? Sometimes I do, but most of the time I do not. Things around me make me sad or I am dissatisfied with myself. But there is a difference between glad and joy. You may be glad but that is superficial; but to rejoice is something that is deep within. As the Bible says, "The joy of the Lord is your strength." It is not the joy that comes from outside such as the joy that comes when you enjoy something tremendously and your soul is satisfied, making you glad, happy, and laughing; but that is transient. When the Lord Himself is your joy, that joy never changes.

When the apostle Paul wrote the Philippian letter, in spite of his terrible, unbearable, unendurable circumstance, in every chapter he mentions the word *joy*. The Philippian believers really loved one another except for two sisters who were in rivalry that cast a sadness over them. If we look at the environment, we will not rejoice always. If we look within ourselves, we do not find joy there. On the other hand, every time we think of the Lord Himself, the joy is there. Nobody can take it away, and this joy becomes our strength. It enables us to go through any kind of circumstance. That is not only the way of life for us but it is the will of God for you and me.

Pray Unceasingly

Prayer is not just something to be done once a day or twice a day or even three times a day. Prayer is something that is going on within us all the time. In other words, we are in touch with heaven.

Give Thanks in All Things

Are we able to do that by ourselves? No. Sometimes we give thanks when we consider what God has bestowed upon us. But most times we are not thankful; especially this generation. But to walk worthy of God's kingdom, He expects us to give thanks in all things—good things and bad things. It is all the same because this is the will of God in Christ Jesus for you. Are we able to do it ourselves? No; but when we look to the

Lord, that is what He is. That is the way we can walk worthy of God's kingdom.

Suffering with Faith

Finally, in II Thessalonians 1:5 the apostle Paul said: "A manifest token of the righteous judgment of God, to the end that ye should be counted worthy of the kingdom of God, for the sake of which ye also suffer." Here we find that they suffered, and suffering with faith is the sure evidence that they had the kingdom. May the Lord use these words to encourage us, to strengthen us, and to press on towards the goal!

Let us pray:

Dear Lord, we do want to praise and thank Thee that from the beginning to the very end, it is Thy grace. There is nothing that we can do except to open our hearts and receive grace upon grace that Thou may be manifested even in our daily walk. Make us worthy of Thy kingdom; and we ask it in Thy precious name. Amen.

QUESTIONS AND ANSWERS

Hebrews 8:11—And they shall not teach each his fellow-citizen, and each his brother, saying, Know the Lord; because all shall know me in themselves, from the little one among them unto the great among them.

This is what the question and answer period is. We are living today in the New Covenant time, and this is one of the chief articles that God has covenanted with us through our Lord Jesus. This tells us that there is no need for anyone to teach another one saying, "Know the Lord." Now this is an objective knowing or a mental knowledge. There is no need for that because we who are in the New Covenant know Him inwardly. We know Him not by the knowledge coming from outside through our mind, but we know Him deep within our spirit. The Holy Spirit who dwells in our spirit will teach us of Christ. This is true from the smallest to the greatest. None is exempted.

Why then do we ask questions? And why are there answers? Let us remember that our soul is so precious before God that He will not and He has not committed any soul to any person in the world. He will only entrust our precious souls to the Holy Spirit. So He alone is our Counselor and our Teacher. However, He does not teach us from the outside but deep within our spirit. He reveals Christ to us through our intuition. So if we want to get a real answer, there is only one way: do not go to man, go to the Lord. As we commune with Him and seek Him, then the Holy Spirit who dwells in us will without any doubt reveal it to us.

Now if this is the case, why do we ask? Let's throw all of the teachers out the window. But we need to remember that because we are still young, we are not too sure what the Spirit of God has revealed to us is right or not. That is the reason why we need some brothers or sisters to help us. Nevertheless, all they can do is confirm or even correct. That is the function of those who teach. Therefore, no teacher should be anxious to teach. Any teacher who is a real teacher should be very reluctant to teach and should give place to the Holy Spirit to speak. Now having said these words we will try to help with some of the questions.

A GUILTY CONSCIENCE

Q: When I have a guilty conscience or am physically weak, what are ways of restoring the worthiness and nearness to God and God's kingdom?

A: Sometimes people may have a guilty conscience. If you have a guilty conscience, of course, your spiritual life is impaired. No one can live a spiritual life with a guilty conscience. Thank God, He has made provision for us as we find in Hebrews 10:22: "Let us approach with a true heart, in full assurance of faith, sprinkled as to our hearts from a wicked conscience, and washed as to our body with pure water."

There is only one way to clear a guilty conscience. You cannot clear it by accumulating merits. The only way is to have your conscience sprinkled with the blood of our Lord Jesus. Only the efficacy of the blood of our Lord Jesus is able to wash your wicked conscience from you. We should not for a moment try to continue on with a wicked conscience. Immediately, when we find our conscience accusing us, we do not wait until evening but go at once to the Lord and ask for the cleansing of His precious blood because it has eternal value. If it can cleanse us before we believe in the Lord, it can continually cleanse us. Those who are very close to God treasure the blood of our Lord Jesus the most. Some people say that even our tears of repentance need to be washed with the blood of the Lord Jesus. That is the only way. Only with a conscience void of offense before God and man can we be strong in the Lord and grow properly in the Lord.

A WEAK BODY

The other part of the question has to do with a weak body. We are a tripartite. In other words, we are made of spirit, soul, and body, but we are one. That is why when we have a weak body, it can affect our spirit by making it weak. Usually when a person has a weak spirit, sometimes he will be under unnecessary condemnation. There is no reason behind it. It is because our spirit is weak, and the only way for a weak conscience to be delivered is through knowledge—real knowledge or true knowledge of God.

On the other hand, it does not necessarily mean that a weak body means a weak spirit. If your body can affect your spirit so much, it means you have not tried by the grace of God to put your body under. Paul said, "I put my body under. I beat it black and blue that it will not have any control over me. On the contrary, I control my weak body. Even if my body is weak, my spirit is strong."

SERVING THE LORD WITH JOY

Q: In the Lord's service, most of the time I feel I am unworthy and unaccomplished. This can be for months and years. How do I know that my services to God are worthy and are bringing glory to Him? How do I serve the Lord always with joy?

A. On the one hand, all who serve the Lord should feel unworthy. If you begin to feel you are worthy, something is terribly wrong. We are serving such a glorious God, we will never be worthy. It is He who makes us worthy; therefore, a sense of gratitude should always be there. When we begin to feel that God should be grateful to us, then something is terribly, terribly wrong. As we are serving, it is to be with a grateful heart knowing that we are so unworthy and the Lord still watches.

Sometimes when we are serving, we analyze it. We try to find out if it is really worthy to the Lord. Has my service really given God the glory? If you are analyzing your service all the time, it simply means you are seeking something for yourself.

How do I know that what I have done is worthy to the Lord? Of course, we need to know His will. If we serve according to our will, we will doubt. Hence, in our serving the Lord we need to hear from the Lord. As a servant the most important thing is the ear—not the hand, mouth, or feet. It is our ear. Learn to hear from the Lord and serve only under His command. It is not just rushing here and there, doing this and that according to what we think God would have. That is a bad servant. A good servant stands before the Lord listening and waiting for the

Lord's command. Once we offer ourselves to the Lord then we stand before Him waiting to hear from Him. After He has shown us the way, we go ahead and serve by the power of the Holy Spirit and leave the result to God. He is the One who will gather us before Him one day and decide whose service is worthy and whose is not.

LIVING WHAT WE SPEAK

Q: I cannot live out the life of Christ within me. What shall I do? What I speak is one thing, how I live is another thing. What shall I do?

A: Thank God, one day we realize that we are not able to live out the life of Christ in us. That is to say, even though we are saved by grace, we are still living by ourselves. We try to be a Christian instead of letting Christ live out His life in us. One thing we have to remember is that there is only one Person who can live a Christian life, and that is Christ Himself. No matter how moral or diligent we may be, no matter how much effort we put into living a Christian life, we are far below the standard of God. Christ alone is the standard, and He lives fully in the will of God. We are trying to do it instead of stepping aside and saying, "Lord, You live in me. I am tired of living by myself. By faith, I believe what You have done on Calvary's cross. I am crucified with Christ, and no longer live I. I live in the flesh, but it is not I; it is Christ who lives in me and I live by His faith" (see Galatians 2:20).

Oftentimes we live by feeling. If I feel good, maybe I am living by Christ and living out His life in me. If I do not feel good, then I am not living by Christ. That is our feeling. It is me, not Christ. Christian life is a life of faith. Therefore, we are to look away from ourselves and look off unto Jesus the Author and Finisher of our faith.

It is true that God expects us to speak in the same measure as we live. That is the rule. He does not want us to say one thing and live another way. That is hypocrisy; it is not true.

However, sometimes—not all the times—we may speak more than what we are. I think probably most teachers and preachers have this experience, and it is because God is leading them on. But this cannot be the rule. Once in a while, we may find that God reveals something to us more than what we really are. Even though we are still learning, God allows us to share it with other people. Nevertheless, when that happens, we have to do it with humility.

THE KINGDOM OF THE HEAVENS—THE KINGDOM OF GOD

Q: Here is a question to be clarified. Why has God planned the kingdom of heaven in addition to the kingdom of God?

A: Of course, we know that this is a misunderstanding. The kingdom of the heavens is part of the kingdom of God. It is included in the kingdom of God because the kingdom of God is from eternity to eternity. Time-wise the kingdom of the heavens seems to be especially related to Christians. This message came from the Lord Jesus at His first coming. He is establishing His kingdom of the heavens upon the earth but it is only to be publically manifested at His second coming during the millennium. Time-wise, it is a section of the kingdom of God specified for Christians.

Matthew 11 says that the kingdom of the heaven is to be taken by violence and the violent seize upon it. We who have believed in the Lord Jesus, who are His disciples, are called to do violence to ourselves. This simply means to deny ourselves, take up the cross, and follow the Lord because this is the reality of the kingdom of the heavens. When the heavens do rule over us, then whatever is earthly or fleshly or of self needs to be denied, and we are to take up the cross and follow Christ.

Those who actually live in the reality of the kingdom of the heavens today, when that kingdom becomes public and is manifested in this world at the second coming of our Lord, then they will be rewarded with ruling and reigning with Christ for a thousand years. Strictly speaking, it is one and the same thing but it is especially related to believers.

HOW THE CHRISTIAN SPIRIT CAN BE DEFILED

Q: You made reference to II Corinthians 7:1 and said that the Christian spirit can be contaminated. How and in what way?

A: It does say in II Corinthian 7:1 to purify your flesh and spirit in the fear of God. In other words, our spirits can be defiled. Once our spirit was defiled by sin to such an extent that it became dead to God; but even now this new human spirit that has been renewed, cleansed, and indwelt by Christ as life and the Holy Spirit as Comforter can be defiled. How? The spirit and the soul are so close that if we live according to our soul-life, sooner or later it will defile our spirit. In other words, it will make our spirits dull. It is as if we are not able to divide or discern what is of the spirit and what is of the soul. It is extremely important that we experience the salvation of the soul and not allow the soul to interfere, to intrude or to inject itself into our spirit, dulling it and defiling it. This is what can happen.

.

Other Books Printed By
Christian Testimony Ministry

Speaker	Title
Dana Congdon	Marriage, Singleness, and the Will of God
	Recovery & Restoration
	The Holy Spirit
	Hebrews
A.J. Flack	Tent of His Splendour
Stephen Kaung	Acts
	Be Ye Therefore Perfect
	Called Out Unto Christ
	Called to the Fellowship of God's Son
	Divine Life and Order
	For Me to Live is Christ
	Glorious Liberty of the Children of God
	God's Purpose for the Family
	I Will Build My Church
	Meditations on the Kingdom
	Recovery
	Spiritual Exercise
	Spiritual Life (II Corinthians Series)
	Teach Us to Pray
	The Cross
	The Fulness of Christ—In the Book of Revelation
	The Headship of Christ
	The Kingdom and the Church
	The Kingdom of God
	The Last Call to the Churches, the Call to Overcome
	The Life of Our Lord Jesus
	The Life of the Church, the Body of Christ
	The Lord's Table
	Two Guideposts for Inheriting the Kingdom
	Vision of Christ (Revelation)
	Who Are We?

SPIRITUAL WARFARE
SPIRITUAL ASCENDANCY
SPIRITUAL MINDEDNESS
SPIRITUAL PERFECTION
SPIRITUAL FULNESS
SPIRITUAL SONSHIP
SPIRITUAL STEWARDSHIP
SPIRITUAL TRAVAIL
SPIRITUAL INHERITANCE
HARVEY CEDARS CONFERENCE:
HILE, KAUNG, LAMBERT
THE KING IS COMING

www.ingramcontent.com/pod-product-compliance
Lightning Source LLC
Chambersburg PA
CBHW060702030426
42337CB00017B/2716